MW01136074

All About Ants

Rosen
REAL
READERS

The Rosen Publishing Group, Inc.
New York

1

Ants are bugs. Most ants are very small. Some ants are so small you can't even see them!

Feelers

Ants have feelers on the tops of their heads. Feelers help ants find food, find their way, or even find other ants.

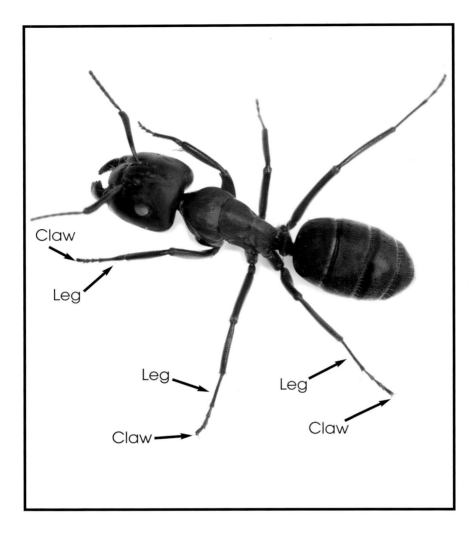

Claw

Leg

Leg

Leg

Claw

Claw

Ants have six legs. Each leg has a claw at the end of it. Ants use their legs and claws to climb and dig.

Jaws

Ants have two sets of jaws. They use one set of jaws to carry things. They use the other set of jaws to chew their food.

5

Most ants eat plants and seeds.
Some ants store leaves in their
nests to eat later.

Some ants eat other bugs.
Army ants hunt in large groups
to catch spiders, beetles, and
even other kinds of ants.

Ants are very strong. They can lift things that are fifty times heavier than they are.

Most ants live in nests that they build in the ground. They use their claws to dig tunnels and make rooms.

Sometimes ants build an anthill around the opening to their nest. An anthill is a pile of dirt that keeps the nest safe.

Ants help farmers. Ants mix and move dirt as they build their nests. This makes the dirt easier for farmers to move when they plant their crops.

Words to Know

anthill

crops

feelers

jaws

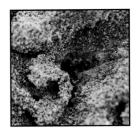

tunnels